CASE
FOR
FAITH
FOR KIDS

Other books in the Lee Strobel series for kids

Case for Christ for Kids,
Updated and Expanded

Case for a Creator for Kids,
Updated and Expanded

NEW YORK TIMES BESTSELLING AUTHOR

LEE STROBEL

WITH ROB SUGGS AND ROBERT ELMER

CASE
FOR
FAITH
FOR KIDS

UPDATED AND
EXPANDED

ZONDER**kidz**

ZONDERKIDZ

Case for Faith for Kids, Updated and Expanded
Copyright © 2006, 2010, 2022 by Lee Strobel and Robert Elmer

Requests for information should be addressed to:
Zonderkidz, 3900 Sparks Dr. SE, Grand Rapids, Michigan 49546

ISBN 978-0-310-77119-7 (softcover)
ISBN 978-0-310-14126-6 (audio download)
ISBN 978-0-310-77120-3 (ebook)

Library of Congress Cataloging-in-Publication Data

Strobel, Lee, 1952-
    Case for faith for kids / Lee Strobel with Rob Suggs and Robert Elmer. —
Updated and expanded.
        p. cm.
    ISBN 978-0-310-71991-5 (softcover)
    1. Apologetics — Juvenile literature. 2. Christian life — Juvenile literature. I.
Suggs, Rob. II. Elmer, Robert. III. Title.
BT1103.S77 2010
    239 — dc22   2009041416

Art direction: Kris Nelson
Cover Design: Jody Langley
Interior Design: Luke Daab and Carlos Estrada
Illustrations copyright © 2010 Terry Colon

Printed in the United States of America

22 23 24 25 26 / LSC / 10 9 8 7 6 5 4 3 2 1

TABLE OF CONTENTS

Introduction:

ANY QUESTIONS?

Hey, do you like questions?
Questions come in lots of different flavors. Of course, there are the boring questions:

- Who was the thirteenth president of the United States?
- What is the state bird of Montana?

  Then there are those corny questions called riddles:

- Why did the chicken cross the playground?

To get to the other slide.

Then there are the head-scratching, noggin-tickling questions:

- Why do we drive on a parkway but park on a driveway?
- Why does "after dark" occur after light?
- Why are whales still chubby after all that swimming?
- Why don't sheep shrink in the rain?
- Why do cameras have round lenses but take square pictures?
- Why does night fall but day break?
- Why do we call one of the hottest dishes "chili"?
- Why are many people afraid of heights, but no one is afraid of widths?

Those questions probably don't have answers, but they're fun to ask anyway.

Then there are questions that *do* have answers. For example, do you ever stand on the beach and wonder how the moon way up *there* causes all those waves way down *here*? Or how long it would take to travel to another galaxy?

We could get those answers without much problem. That's why we have science. The kind of science called *physics* would tell us about the moon and tides. *Astronomy* would tell us about how long to plan for an intergalactic vacation.

BIG-LEAGUE QUESTIONS

Then there are those questions that everyone wonders about at some time or another:

How did this world get here?

Is there a God?

Which religion is true?

In case you're interested, a book called *Case for a Creator* works on the God question. Another one called *Case for Christ* covers questions about Jesus, such as: Was he really the Son of God? Could he really have risen from the dead?

This book is filled with big-league questions about believing in God and following Christ. A lot of Christians wonder about these noggin-nibblers:

- If God is good, why does he let bad things happen in the world?
- Do miracles happen or does science prove they are impossible?
- Is Jesus the only way to get into heaven? What about other religions?
- If I have questions or doubts, does that mean I'm not a Christian?

WHY ASK IN THE FIRST PLACE?

Those are some brain-drainers! People ask these questions all the time, and why shouldn't they? The answers are very important. It's only natural that folks would wonder.

And here's one more question: Should people who already believe in God ask for answers? If they wonder, for instance, whether God is really fair, does that mean they don't trust God enough? Should they just ignore the tough stuff and go on believing in God?

No, because questions — especially questions about faith — are too important to let us do that. Whether you believe in God or not, it's a pretty good idea to give these questions some thought. Look at it this way: people have worked on these riddles for thousands of years, and they haven't proved yet that God isn't alive. So what do you have to lose?

Not your faith. Faith is like a muscle that just becomes stronger the more you put it to work. Proverbs 18:17 tells us, "The first one to tell his case seems right. Then someone else comes forward and questions him." That's just a fancy way of saying it's important to carefully ask the right questions to get the right clues — don't be too quick to jump to conclusions. Then you can make up your own mind about the truth.

ASK. SEARCH. KNOCK.

Jesus said this: "Ask, and it will be given to you. Search, and you will find. Knock, and the door will be opened to you. Everyone who asks will receive. He who searches will find. The door will be opened to the one who knocks" (Matthew 7:7–8).

Ask, search, and knock. Why?

Imagine trying to find an old friend who moved away from the neighborhood. How would you go about it? First, you would *ask*. "Anybody know where my friend's new house is?" Maybe someone at school would say, "I heard that kid lives over near the park now."

What would you do next? You would *search*. Maybe you'd get on your bike and ride to the park to look for your friend. Finally, what would you do when you found the right house? You would *knock*. Then you could see your friend face-to-face.

1. Ask
2. Search
3. Knock

That's why we ask questions about God. It's a way of finding him for ourselves. Asking leads us to search for him more actively, and searching for him makes it possible to meet him.

> Remember, even though it's important to ask questions about God to find him, he is always searching for you.

In this verse, God's talking: "When you look for me with all your heart, you will find me" (Jeremiah 29:13). That means to seek with your best effort.

That sounds like a good idea. It's time to really go after these questions. If you ask and think and search for the answers with all your heart, maybe you'll finally discover that every answer leads to God himself. Because, as Saint Augustine said, "All truth is God's truth."

So tighten your thinking cap, march boldly to the next page, and prepare yourself to do some thinking and maybe even have some fun doing it. We're going to tackle five big-time questions, one by one.

Part 1
CASE FOR FAITH

Chapter 1

WHY WOULD A GOOD GOD ALLOW BAD THINGS?

Early on August 29, 2005, Hurricane Katrina hit the Gulf Coast of the United States.

People in the city of New Orleans, Louisiana, were on alert. At first it seemed as if the winds had done little damage. But the next morning, the storm walls, called levees, burst. Seawater swirling wildly from the storm washed across the city. Hundreds of thousands of people lost their homes and had to flee the city. But some couldn't leave because they were sick, handicapped, elderly, or didn't have transportation.

Many people died from the tragic flooding. Survivors flocked to the Louisiana Superdome, the enclosed stadium that had been built for games and fun. It soon became a crowded place of pain and panic. No one had enough water or food. There were no working bathrooms. Families were separated in the confusion.

Then came more tragedy, caused not by wind or water but by people. Criminals showed up on the flooded streets, breaking into buildings and stealing all they could carry. There were violent attacks, some against soldiers and rescuers who came to help. People fought viciously for seats on

There were also heroes who helped others in need of food and shelter. Did you know that military troops and volunteers from all over the country traveled down to the Gulf to help clean up the city, hand out food and water, and rescue survivors? The helpers spent many sleepless nights and made great sacrifices to help out in any way they could.

the buses in order to escape a city of terror that had once been home, a vacation destination, and a place of good food and parties.

People all over the world began to ask questions. How could *nature* be so cruel? How could *people* behave with even more cruelty at the very worst time?

And where was God when we needed him most? Wasn't he watching out for the world? Couldn't he have stopped the storm? Couldn't he have protected innocent victims from flooding and criminals?

Question: Have you heard about a disaster like Katrina, the earthquake in Haiti in January 2010, or perhaps some fire or accident in your town? Did you see pictures on television? How did you feel when you saw the pictures or heard the stories? Why?

AN ANCIENT QUESTION

Ever since the earth has had people living on it, these great questions have been asked: Where is God when bad things happen? Why won't he protect us from disaster? Why doesn't he punish the bad people? Deep thinkers call these questions the problem of evil. They wonder why there is evil at all if our world is guarded by a God who cares about us.

If we have a good God, why do bad things happen?

That last question really takes some tough thinking. A Greek philosopher named Epicurus asked it more than two thousand years ago. It seemed to him that if God and evil are both in the world, then God should use his powers to eliminate it. If he doesn't, the philosopher asked, why doesn't he? Does he lack the desire or does he lack the strength?

Problem of evil: questions people ask when bad things happen. The questions are about why God didn't save or help people when they were in trouble.

That's a tough one! Christians believe God is as good as it is possible to be, *and* as strong as it is possible to be. But if Epicurus were here, he would reply, "Then why does he let bad things happen in the world?"

How would you answer his question? This one's harder than math! For now, let's just understand what Epicurus (and many other people throughout the ages) asked. As you continue your journey throughout this book, you'll learn the best answers for these questions. Fair enough?

Question: When you think of God, do you think more of power or love? Why?

GOD AND CHEATERS

You don't need a hurricane to make this question important. Imagine you're sitting in your desk at school when you see Chad, the kid over in the second row, sneaking his test answers from a tiny piece of paper in his watchband. On top of that, Chad has all the latest video games, and his parents give him everything he wants.

Then you think of Jenny, who sits in the back row. A hard worker, she's nice to everyone. But

she comes from a poor family; she owns just two sets of school clothes. Yet Jenny is a really great person, and would never cheat on a test or be unkind to anyone.

After a while, you begin to wonder why life works out like that. Sometimes the least deserving kids have the best setup. Again, what about God? If he has the power, why doesn't he give Jenny the break she deserves — and maybe even teach Chad a lesson?

The prophet Jeremiah asked God about this deal. "But now I would like to speak with you about whether you are being fair. Why are sinful people successful? Why do those who can't be trusted have an easy life?" (Jeremiah 12:1).

Question: What kinds of "unfair" things have you noticed at school or in the neighborhood? Why do you think some people do wrong things?

LET'S ASK THE EXPERTS

Peter Kreeft is a smart man — he teaches philosophy at Boston College. He has done a lot of reading and a lot of thinking about the problem of evil. Imagine you're a reporter trying to stump him with some tough questions.

You: Why would God create evil in the first place?

Peter: Well, my answer would be that God didn't create evil.

You: Okay, then who did?

Peter: *We* did. By that I mean that God made *people*. And when he did, he gave them the ability to make decisions in life. That's called "free choice."

You: But what about evil?

Peter: Evil is what happens when people use their free choice in the wrong way. People can choose to love, but they often choose to hurt each other instead. That's what evil is: the decision to do the wrong thing. God doesn't make that decision — we do.

You: You're not getting off that easy. Why didn't God make us *unable* to hate or to hurt?

Peter: Let's say you have a doll with a little button that makes the doll say, "I love you." Over and over. Is that a great toy or what?

You: No way! It's boring!

Peter: Exactly. If God had made us with no choice,

we would be like plastic dolls that couldn't do anything but say "I love you" over and over. That's not really love because we'd be forced to say it. But we don't have any buttons. We *choose* to obey God or not. When we decide to please him because we want to, not because we *have* to — well, that means something. God doesn't care about dolls, but about real people who make real choices.

THE CHOICE IS YOURS

Professor Kreeft is saying that if we could *only* do good stuff, we would be like robots — just lifeless toys that God was playing with.

Think of it another way. Why play soccer? If you play, you could lose! But you play because the fun makes the risk of losing worthwhile, right? If you knew for sure that you would win *every* single game, would winning mean as much or feel as good? Of course not.

People can hurt God's feelings, Professor K. says. God made us that way because he wanted real, thinking friends instead of boring dolls or robots. Friendship is worth the risk of disappointment just as soccer is worth the risk of losing. So, according to Professor K., God created *choice*. People came up with the evil part.

Okay. Evil is something people do. But wait just a minute! What about the *other* kind of evil? Some evil is not personal, but *natural* — that is, brought about by nature. There are hurricanes, earthquakes, famines, and diseases that make innocent people suffer. Nobody chooses a disaster. So what's up with that?

DISEASES AND DISASTERS

Some of those deep thinkers feel that natural disasters such as Hurricane Katrina raise much tougher questions about God, because in disaters people seem to suffer for no good reason. We can't just blame people.

Christians find a consistent answer to this question in the Bible. God's children were actually perfect in every way before people chose to disobey him. Disobedience is called "sin." Sinning caused humans to be imperfect, and thus also caused the earth to be imperfect. God said, "I am putting a curse on the ground because of what you did" (Genesis 3:17). Through poor choices, people and the world were damaged. Therefore, there are diseases and disasters.

One Christian thinker, Cliffe Knechtle, put it this way: "When we humans told God to shove off, he partially honored our request. Nature began to revolt. The earth was cursed. Genetic breakdown and disease began. Pain and death became part of the human experience."

All of God's creation, therefore, is hurting. It is "groaning," according to Romans 8:22. That's the bad news. The good news is, things are going to get better! "The creation looks forward to the day when it will join God's children in glorious freedom from death and decay" (Romans 8:21 NLT). What does that mean? God has a plan to restore perfection to both the people and the planet.

Payback or Proving Ground?

One day Jesus and his friends met a man who had been blind since birth. They began to discuss whether his blindness was God's punishment for the man's sinful behavior, or whether it was payback for something his parents had done. (In those days, many people believed that disabilities were punishment for wrongdoing.)

Jesus said both views were wrong. It was actually "so that God's work could be shown" (John 9:3). Now there's an idea! No one likes problems, but we can look at them as a chance to show the difference God can make in our problems.

Evil, then, is not just a problem – it's an opportunity to make something good out of a tough situation.

SO WHY DOESN'T GOD DO SOMETHING NOW?

There is at least one good reason God doesn't snap a heavenly finger and make all the bad things go away. It's easier to understand when you think about how parents raise their children.

Mom watches Timmy every moment when Timmy is a baby. But as Timmy gets a little older, she allows him to play outside — even out of her sight when he reaches a certain age. What if he falls down and skins a knee? He just might, but Mom knows that Timmy must eventually learn how to care for himself, and she will hear him if he calls for her. Besides, what would Timmy's life be like if his mother followed him everywhere, protecting him even when he became a teenager? Timmy would hate it!

What if your parents never let you ride a bicycle because they knew that you would take a few tumbles while learning? If they want you to have all the fun of bike-riding, they have to let you experience a few bumps and bruises.

God allows us to suffer sometimes because there is a lesson for us to learn — and because of one other cool idea found in the Bible, in Romans chapter 8.

ALL FOR THE BEST

"We know that in all things God works for the good of those who love him."
(Romans 8:28)

That's one amazing verse. It says that no matter what happens, God is going to bring something good out of it for his followers! *Can he do that?* Well, after all, he *is* God.

As amazing as it seems, this happens all the time. The Gulf Coast hurricane is one example. Within a few days of the tragedy, people all over the United States were offering to help. Some of them opened their homes for victims of the disaster to come stay with them. People gave food, clothing, money, and new houses. Some kids gave up all their birthday presents to let the money be used for helping those in need.

Whenever bad things happen, good people seem to come from every direction, ready to help. Maybe God sends them. Maybe he's not ignoring people's problems after all.

Question: Have you ever helped people in need? Have you heard stories of people who helped after a disaster? How did that make you feel?

YEAH, BUT EVIL IS STILL UNFAIR!

Still worried about tragedies and innocent children who die of starvation? You should be! There is no simple answer for the question of why innocent people suffer. The ideas in this chapter help, but that doesn't make evil any less evil. Just because you might see how God works does *not* mean that disasters and diseases are good in any way.

It *does* mean that no matter how dark the world may become, God's light is brighter still. The Bible also says there will be a time when there will be no more darkness or evil at all — in human nature or in the world.

"We are looking forward to a new heaven and a new earth. Godliness will make its home there. All of this is in keeping with God's promise" (2 Peter 3:13).

Chapter 2

DOES SCIENCE MEAN MIRACLES CAN'T HAPPEN?

H i there, Levi. How was your day? Eat all your lunch?"

"Nope, Mom. Shared it with a few friends."

"Well, that was nice. Which friends would that be?"

"Don't know all their names."

"*All* their names? You just had one fish sandwich. How many friends did you share it with?"

"Five thousand."

Silence.

"Levi, what have we told you about telling fibs?"

"I'm not fibbing! Folks were hungry. Teacher said to share. I shared."

"Levi, that comes out to — um, five thousand eaters, half a crumb per person. No way."

"*Way.* Actually, everyone chowed down until they were stuffed."

"Leeeeeeeeviii …"

"Um … Mom?"

"What now?"

"Where should I put this basket of leftovers?"

This made-up story was based on a true one you can read in Matthew 14. People didn't have much understanding of science in the time of Christ, but even so, Levi's mom understood that sandwiches answer to certain physical laws, and sandwiches are pretty law-abiding in that regard. Meaning, you can split a fish sandwich only so many ways.

These days, people take science for granted. You can watch something on your television set as it is happening on the other side of the world. You can fly through the sky in an airplane. A century or two ago, such things would have seemed greater miracles than five thousand dudes sharing a trout-burger. But we know that television and air flight are just matters of science.

But that raises another big-league question. If science can explain so many things, does that mean there are no real miracles?

The reason that's such a big question is if there is only science (natural) and nothing miraculous (supernatural), where does that leave God? You can't see him through a microscope or a telescope, after all. In the Bible, he used miracles to show he was real. So what's the deal? Can miracles happen? And if not, does that mean there is no God?

Or is there some way both science and miracles can be true?

Question: Do you think miracles happen today? If you could ask God to perform one miracle, what would it be? Why?

ASK THE PHILOSOPHER

Put your reporter hat on again. Time to take a little trip.

You're climbing a mountain in the mysterious Himalayas. Snow whips around your body as you try to make your way to the top. The wind howls as you reach the crest where a philosopher sits — a wise guru, thinking deep thoughts about the meaning of life. His lengthy beard spills around his bare feet, and a hood covers his eyes. His name is Bill Craig.

(Okay. So the mountain stuff is made up. Bill Craig is a real guy, but he wears a tie and sits around in an office drinking coffee. This book needed a little mystery and adventure, okay?)

You: Dude. You're a deep guy. A thinking guy. A science guy.

Bill: Well, I like to think so.

You: But you're a faith guy too?

Bill: Definitely. I believe in Jesus with all my heart.

You: So how did that happen? Jesus is all about miracles and the supernatural, right?

Bill: I became a Christian because I cared about Jesus. I have experienced him, just like I would "experience" something in science or regular life. You don't have to have all your questions answered to come to faith. You just have to say, "The weight of the evidence seems to show this is true, so even though I don't have answers to all my questions, I'm going to believe and hope for answers in the long run." That's what happened with me. And the more I've seen the evidence of science and history, the more it has strengthened my faith.

You: Well, if you believe in science, what do you do when the Bible tells you that Jesus fed five thousand people with a little bread and fish?

Bill: What I do is figure that if Jesus is God, as he says he is, he can do what he wants. He made the universe, so what's the big deal about feeding a few extra people? Or walking on water? Or rising from the dead, for that matter? God made science, not the other way around.

You: Still, doesn't he have to break the laws of science — mess up his own system — to perform a miracle?

Bill: Not the way I look at it. Let's say an apple is about to fall from the tree. The laws of science (gravity, actually) say it will hit the ground. But I step up and catch the apple. Have I broken the laws of science? The answer is no, I haven't. I have stepped in and *intervened*. A miracle is when God steps in and does something in the world. It's *super*natural — that means it's not *against* nature but *higher* than nature.

Even though miracles might seem supernatural to us, they aren't to God. They're just part of God's ability to reach out to us.

Chapter 3
THE BIG FIVE

As you nervously climb back down the mountain, searching for a foothold as the wind rages (just play along, you're on a roll), you carry a piece of paper that the guru handed to you. You had said, "Okay, Mr. Philosopher, if you're so smart, give me five good reasons to believe in God when science explains so much."

He said, "No problem," and pulled out this handy slip of paper with five points on it. You decided to read it when you got to the bottom of the page — um, the mountain.

FIVE REASONS GOD MAKES SENSE EVEN WITH SCIENCE

1. God makes sense of creation.

Many scientists today believe that the universe began with a "big bang." All matter — every particle that existed — was together before exploding outward. The explosion, still in progress, created every star, every planet, and everything else in space.

But what made the bang?

No matter how much we discover about that first explosion that brought the universe into being, we must agree that some force beforehand set it all in motion. After all, whatever begins to exist has a cause. If the universe began to exist at some

God has always existed. He never had a beginning, so he doesn't need a cause to exist.

point in the past, then it must have had a cause. What could that cause have been? God makes the most sense.

(And what caused God to exist? Well, unlike the universe, he never had a beginning, so he
doesn't need a cause!)

2. *God makes sense of the fine details of life.*

Scientists are learning a lot about how stuff
works in our universe. They're discovering more
about how gravity pulls us to earth, what it takes
for us to be able to live and breathe on a planet
like ours — things like that.

These same scientists have been amazed at
what they have found. For example, a famous
scientist named Stephen Hawking figured out
that the big bang happened in *exactly, absolutely,
precisely* the right way for there to even *be* a
universe. If the speed of the bang had been faster or
slower by one part in a hundred thousand *million
million*, the whole thing would have collapsed into
a fireball! Who could have fine-tuned the whole
thing to make sure that didn't happen?

Or think about this one, worked out by a
scientist named P. C. W. Davies. If the force of
gravity were weaker *or* stronger by one part in
a number we don't have room to write here (10
with one hundred zeros after it!), then there
never could have been life on this earth.

Imagine someone sprinkling enough salt to

cover the entire surface of a football field. There is one specific grain of salt that is the "special" one (though it looks like every other grain of salt). How likely would it be that you could walk out there and select *that very grain* without help? Not much chance, right?

The force of gravity is set at one specific measurement that is just as precise. It could have been any other measurement, just like any of those other grains of salt. Could it have just worked out exactly right without someone "helping" to select the right measurement?

In other words, who could have fine-tuned the force of gravity? Think about it the next time you drop your ice-cream cone.

Who sits at the controls and sets all the dials? Faith in God makes sense when you look at the details of life.

Try It Yourself!

Got a deck of cards? Build a house with them. Prop up four cards for your walls, then put on a ceiling.

Now that you've mastered a simple shack, try a mansion. Add several more packs of cards. Build some large rooms and make your home seven or eight stories high. Can you do it? How about a skyscraper?

As you can see, you have to be able to balance every single card perfectly in relation to every single other card. Because just when you get everything to barely balance, adding another card throws everything off and makes the whole house fall down – unless you have superhuman balancing skills.

Scientists say the universe is like an almost infinitely high skyscraper of cards, each card (or physical condition) arranged so delicately in relation to every other one that if you pulled out one card, the house would collapse.

The Bible says that Jesus "created everything in heaven and on earth. He created everything that can be seen and everything that can't be seen ... He holds everything together" (Colossians 1:16 - 17).

3. God makes sense of right and wrong.

Have you ever thought about where the ideas of "right" and "wrong" come from? Some ideas are opinions, such as whether red is a better color than blue. We all know there are no right or wrong answers for color preference; it just depends on who is being asked. But when it comes to stealing and murder, most people all over the world agree that these things are wrong. Why? Who decides that certain things are right or wrong?

If you think about it, if there were no God, every idea would just be an opinion. You couldn't say that murdering or stealing were "just wrong, period." It would be like red or blue, chocolate or vanilla — one answer would be as good as the other.

Once you decide that certain things are always right or always wrong, then what you are saying is that there is something like an "honor code" for the whole world — even for the universe. Does your school have an honor code, telling students how they must behave? Someone had to write it — maybe the principal, the teachers, or a group of parents. Rules don't write themselves. But if the universe has its own "honor code" — that is, its own set of rules saying what is right and what is wrong — then those can't have written themselves, either. Could God be the one who made the rules?

Question: If you were the King of the world, what rules for right and wrong would you set? Make a list, and think about why each rule would be on your list. If God were making the rules for us, which would be most important to him? Why?

4. God makes sense of Jesus.

Remember, the subject for this chapter is miracles. If there is a God, then you have to admit that miracles are really no big deal! After all, someone who made the universe can do anything else he wants.

The claim that Jesus rose from the dead is a good example. That would definitely qualify as a miracle, right? But how do you know it happened? Some people insist that the story of Jesus coming back from the dead is a fairy tale, like the story of the Three Bears or Cinderella.

Here are some facts to consider about the death and resurrection of Jesus:

- Everyone knew where he was buried, and the grave was guarded by Roman soldiers.
- Jesus' friends *and* enemies agreed that the body disappeared in only three days.
- Many people saw and talked with a living Jesus in the days that followed.
- The disciples were certain he had risen from the dead — so certain they were willing to give their lives for telling others about it.

All of these points were known just a few

years after the events, when an early Christian named Paul wrote about them. Anyone who knew these to be lies could have said so. But more people wrote about Jesus rising from the dead because he appeared before them. Thousands of others began coming forward to become Christians. Something remarkable surely happened.

If Jesus rose from the dead, then the work of God is the best explanation.

5. God makes sense of our personal experiences.

What if your friend told you that the president of the United States was in the next room? It might be pretty hard to believe, but you could check it out. You could listen at the door — could you recognize his voice? You could ask others in the room if they knew anything about the president visiting your home. But what would be the smartest way to find out? Go and see!

When it comes to the question of God, many people have gone and seen. They have sought God and, they claim, become his friend. This includes many scientists. When you know someone as a friend, you have no more questions about whether they are real. This is still the most convincing point of all.

WHO IS AT THE DOOR?

As you've seen, scientists and other people have gone looking for God. But the good news is that he comes looking for people first. He is looking for you too. How can you know him?

Jesus said, "Here I am! I stand at the door and knock. If any of you hears my voice and opens the door, I will come in and eat with you. And you will eat with me" (Revelation 3:20). That means he expects you to listen for his knock in everyday life. Letting him in means accepting his friendship.

That's when the really cool miracles begin!

Question: Do you have a friendship with God? How is it like other friendships? How is it different? What are some ways that you can make your relationship with God into an even deeper and closer friendship?

Chapter 4

CAN OTHER RELIGIONS GET US INTO HEAVEN?

I magine a giant pyramid, a little like the Great Pyramid of Egypt. But this one has more than four sides. And each side has steps leading upward to its peak, where all the lines come together. One side is marked "Christianity" at the bottom. Many people are eagerly climbing those steps. The next side is marked "Hinduism." It too claims a huge number of devoted climbers. After that comes the side marked "Buddhism," then one marked "Islam."

There are many other sides too, though they are smaller and have fewer people climbing their steps.

At the top of the pyramid, God waits with a big smile. He shakes each person's hand as they reach the top, and he gives that person a ticket to heaven.

But a Buddhist says, "Wait a minute! I did a lot of thinking and reading before choosing my side of the pyramid. I gotta know — was Buddhism the best way or not?"

God shrugs and says, "Oh, all these religions are about the same."

A Christian joins the conversation. "The same? How can that be? I made a comparison, and there were *big* differences."

God says, "Hey, I don't sweat the small stuff. I figure, whatever beliefs work for you are cool with me."

A Hindu says, "But wait — some people said there's *one* of you, while others said there are a *bunch* of gods. Some said there's one lifetime for people on earth, while others said we get a bunch of chances. Are you going to announce the right answers?"

God holds up a hand and says, "Hey, I don't make the rules ... Tickets! Tickets for all!"

Does this seem like a strange picture of God?

Sure, it's a little goofy, but many people today hold to something like that view. They think the world's religions are basically equal. They think the differing views of God, the world, and proper behavior aren't worth worrying about. They believe that truth is whatever anyone decides it is, like chocolate versus vanilla — and that anyone who claims to have the *right* answer is stuck-up.

Even though not everyone is a Christian, it's important to show kindness to people of all faiths. In a book called *Mere Christianity,* a writer named C.S. Lewis said, "There are people in other religions who are being led by God's secret influence to concentrate on those parts of their religion which are in agreement with Christianity, and who thus belong to Christ without knowing it."

So what should we do with the words of Jesus? He is on the record as saying, "I am the way ... No one comes to the Father except through me" (John 14:6). He claims to hold the exclusive ticket to heaven, and he says that everyone must walk on *his* side of the pyramid.

Is that fair? It's a tough question, isn't it? Is there only one way to heaven? Many ways? No way? Is the answer important?

Question: As you read the pyramid story, what do you think about its view of God and religion? What seems right or wrong about it to you?

THAT'S THE TICKET!

Imagine you want to go to that big new theme park, the one with the wild roller coaster called the Nauseator. Since it's Saturday, tickets are sold out, but there are various people walking around outside the gates selling pre-bought tickets. You and your friends are bargaining with some of them, trying to get the best price on tickets.

But you've heard that some of the tickets are fakes! They look real, but they are clever copies of the real thing. At the park gate, the ticket-takers will point special scanners at the tickets and reveal them to be worthless — and some kids will go home disappointed and missing a bunch of money.

We'd all agree that with amusement park tickets, it's important to know the real ones from the fakes. The same can be applied to religion. Isn't it an even bigger deal with religions other than Christianity? Is it a good idea to simply assume that all the "tickets" to heaven are authentic? And if so, how can we tell which ones will get us in the front gate?

ALL CREATED EQUAL?

Some people say that all religions are about the same, but that's actually not true. Ready to play the reporter again? Time to talk to an expert on world religions and find out why. His name is Dr. Paul Copan, and he has worked on over forty books about big topics having to do with faith.

You: So what is really different about all the other world's religions?

Paul: A lot of religions say similar things, like we have to be kind to others or sacrifice things for a greater good. But there are some big differences, and those differences often go against each other. For example, Islam believes Jesus didn't die on the cross, Buddhism doesn't believe there is a creator God, and some Hindus believe that everything around us is God, including them. So not every religion can be telling the truth. And that is what we need to look at—what religion matches up with what we can prove is true?

You: So how can we know Christianity is true?

Paul: Something is true if it matches up with what's real. For example, if I say the earth is round, it's true because we've seen pictures and know it through science. When Jesus was on earth, he said that believing in him and what

he said was the only way to God. And everything Jesus said and did—including his dy-
ing on the cross and rising from the dead—is
backed up by evidence.

Plus, even people who didn't believe in
Jesus at first when he was alive changed their
minds when they saw everything Jesus had
said would happen actually happened.

You: So should Christians tell everyone else they're
wrong?

Paul: We have to be careful about how we talk to
other people about our faith, because they
may be turned off from Christianity if we
say our religion is the best and theirs is bad.
And the Bible tells us not to boast about our
faith or act in ways that make Christians look
judgmental.

You: Does that mean we should just mind our own
business, then?

Paul: No, not at all. When we have an opportunity,
we should tell other people about Jesus and
then let them make up their minds based on
the truths we share. And when we talk to
people who have different beliefs than us, we
should be humble and show grace to them so
they see Jesus' love in us and want to learn
more about being a Christian.

OKAY, SO WHY ISN'T EVERYBODY A CHRISTIAN?

Here's a question to consider: If Christianity is the true religion, why doesn't everybody find that out and switch to Christianity or become a Christian?

For one thing, of course, many people are born in countries where certain religions have been popular for thousands of years. There are many Buddhists in China and Japan, many Hindus in India and surrounding countries, and many Muslims in Middle Eastern countries. In the United States, more than eight out of ten people say they're Christians. So people tend to adopt the religions of their homelands.

Remember what C.S. Lewis wrote about on page 61? What does he say about showing kindness to people of all faiths?

Still, in today's world, where there is more travel and more discussion between people from different cultures, people take new forms of faith at times. Missionaries, including Christian ones, are active in spreading their beliefs to other countries.

Some people reject Christianity because it's demanding. Jesus calls upon us to be unselfish

and to treat others as if they were more important than ourselves. Some people don't want to
try living that way.

Question: Following Jesus means
learning to live unselfishly, to pray for enemies,
and to avoid striking back at people who hurt us.
If a friend told you that for those reasons
Christianity wasn't worth it, what would you tell
him or her?

WHAT ABOUT PEOPLE WHO HAVEN'T HEARD?

One more difficult question. People often ask if it's fair for Christians, and Christians alone, to be allowed into heaven. What if a child is born in a country where few people are Christians? What if she lives her whole life and never hears about Jesus? Would it be fair to exclude her from heaven? One answer might . . .

Paul: Excuse me. May I reply? This is a big topic!

You: Sure! Go ahead and do your thing.

Paul: The Bible tells us that God is kind and loving, and that he doesn't want anyone to miss out on heaven. So he does everything he can to make sure people know him—through missionaries and everyday people who share their faith with others, and by showing us who he is through experiences that point to God being real. Plus, the Holy Spirit is seeking out people as well, working on their hearts. If someone wants to know God, he will help them learn more about him and show them the truths they need to believe.

You: It sounds like God cares a lot about every human being. But what about people who die before knowing about God and Christianity, or have been taught Christianity is wrong?

Paul: Some people who have studied the Bible think that God makes sure that even if someone dies before ever hearing the truth about Christianity, they will have one last chance after they die to decide if they believe it or not. But even if there isn't an after-death chance, we also know from the Bible that God would never do anything that is unfair. That means he'll make sure everyone will have a chance to become a Christian and enter heaven if they truly want to, no matter how it happens.

Question: God says that if we seek him with all our hearts, we will find him. What are some ways of seeking him? Do you want God to know you, as described by Paul Copan? Explain or think about your feeling.

Chapter 5

CAN I HAVE DOUBTS AND STILL BE A CHRISTIAN?

P retend you have a friend named Jason. You want his opinion about what you've been reading so far in this book. Imagine he's been reading this book too.

You: What do you think about all this, Jason? Do you have a question?

Jason: Not one question. A *lot* of them. Or at least ... What I'm trying to say is that I'm still not too sure about all this God stuff. Even after all these ideas and experts and stuff, I don't feel like my faith is very strong.

You: Jason, most people are like you at one time or another. The truth is that if it were *easy* to have faith, it wouldn't be called "faith." It would be called "being sure."

Jason: Okay, so I like to be sure. Is that so wrong? If I'm on a skateboard, I like to be sure the wheels aren't going to fly off when I'm cruising at high speed. If I'm going to make a big deal about God in my life, why shouldn't I be sure about that too?

You: Good point! Think about that one.

Another word for faith is *trust*. Some things are easy to trust — that the sun will come up tomorrow, or that doing homework will help your grades. Seeing is believing, and you've seen those things happen and built your trust on what you've seen.

COMMITMENT:
Another part of trust is commitment. This means agreeing to do something in the future, like your homework or reading the Bible.

But when it comes to questions about God, people are asked to be "sure of what we hope for ... being certain of what we do not see" (Hebrews 11:1). That's hard to do, isn't it?

Jesus had a friend named Thomas who was just like Jason. Even after his friends had told him that Jesus had risen from death, he needed to see with his own eyes before he could believe. When Thomas did see Jesus face-to-face, he bowed before him in faith. Jesus said, "You believe because you see me. Those who believe without seeing me will be truly happy" (John 20:29 NCV).

Truly happy. Cool. Jesus seems to be saying that life is good when we can believe without demanding absolute proof. In other words, faith is an awesome gift.

But does that mean believing anything and everything? Of course not. Jesus isn't suggesting that you'll be truly happy if you convince yourself that all your teachers at school are aliens from outer space, or that you can learn to fly by flapping your arms. True faith is about managing to believe what already happens to be true. It's a step taken in the same direction that the evidence points.

So you look at your skateboard. Will the wheels come flying off if you trust it at high speeds? It's one thing to just hope they won't. It's another thing when your older brother, who's good with fix-it stuff, says, "Hey, I've checked it. The wheel axles are solid!"

That's more than just hope. That's moving ahead based on trusting solid evidence.

So faith is cool. It's based on something *solid.* But doubt is *not* uncool — it actually makes us work on our faith. Make sense? It's all about learning to live with both. It's time to figure out how to do that.

Question: Can you remember when someone fooled you by getting you to believe something that wasn't true? How can you decide whether to believe someone's claim?

WHAT FAITH ISN'T

Some people believe that if they have faith, they should *feel* something. They think that if God lives inside them, they should feel different — like feeling full after dinner or feeling cold in the winter. They wonder why they don't "feel" their faith.

But feeling full or cold is a *physical* feeling. Some feelings are emotions, and they can be fussy or not quite right at times! They change like the weather, and sometimes they don't agree with our *deeper* feelings. Imagine having a terrible argument with your sister outdoors. Right at that moment, you feel like you could clobber her! But imagine that ten seconds later, your sister almost steps in front of a speeding car. Your emotions would quickly change to alarm. You would realize that you love your sister, even when you want to clobber her.

Emotions come and go, and they don't always tell the whole story, do they?

Faith is like love — you can have it without feeling it. You can believe in God even when it feels like he is far away. It's even possible to love God when you're angry with him!

FAITH AND DOUBT ARE FRIENDS

It's also true that faith and doubt are not natural enemies. Actually, those two get along pretty well together.

One day a man came to Jesus with a son who needed healing. Jesus told the father that everything is possible for someone who believes. The man said, "I do believe! Help me overcome my unbelief!" (Mark 9:24). Now, there's something — a man who says that he believes and he doesn't believe. That's kind of like ... well, pretty much all of us. It's not that we have *no* faith. We just want God to help us with those little unfaithful parts inside us.

You will find that there are many people who have been Christians for a lot of years. They continue in their faith, and they continue in their doubts too.

Jason: Excuse me.

You: Oh — Jason! I almost forgot you!

Jason: I noticed. I wanted to ask how come those old-and-wise Christian types still have doubts. Shouldn't they have patched up all the holes in their faith by now?

You: That would be like getting so muscular, you didn't need to lift any more weights. You could always be at least a little stronger, right? Same way with believing. Doubt is the "heavy lifting" of faith. That is, faith is a kind of spiritual muscle you have to exercise by stretching it, working on it, and hammering it until it's tough. Doubt does that.

Jason: Um, I don't get it.

You: Well, let's say you doubt that Jesus rose from the dead. So you go and do a lot of reading about it. If you can disprove it, you'll be the first guy in two thousand years to succeed. If you can't, well, you'll have stronger faith! You've just pumped some spiritual iron.

Question: If you could ask God one question about spiritual things, what question would you ask? If you could name one area where you have some doubts, what would it be?

WORK THOSE MUSCLES!

Okay, so doubt can be like a faith workout. It's kind of heavy and tiring, but it makes you stronger. What are some guidelines for a bout with doubt? Or to put the question another way: Are there more ways you can get stronger in your faith?

Glad you asked that question!

1. Take one giant step.

Sometimes people believe something mostly because they *want* to — or they disbelieve it for the same reason. If someone tells you that your best friend said something bad about you, you don't want to believe it. You might choose then and there to disbelieve. Of course, you'll want to discover the truth by asking some questions.

But you see the point: the desire to believe something has an influence over what people end up believing and doing. You can begin in your faith by making a decision to believe. Does that mean a blind, unthinking decision? Should you put the names of the world's religions in a hat, pick one out at random, and make a decision to follow it?

No way! Faith is never blind. Someone once defined faith in this way: "Faith is walking to the edge of all the light that you have and taking one more step." That step comes when you make a conscious decision to go forward. If the step you're taking is in the same direction that the evidence is pointing — as with Christianity — then that's a logical and rational direction to go.

2. Follow the faithful.

You: Yo, Jason.

Jason: Reporting for duty.

You: What do you think about taking that giant step?

Jason: Um ... Sorry, I missed that one. I was off lifting weights. Thanks for reminding me, dude! I about cramped my left triceps big-time. Feel this knot ...

You: Later, okay? Question: If you want to build your faith, where should you go, other than to the fitness center?

Jason: Um, I'd say ... off to some place in the wilderness, like, to meditate? Maybe in a cave?

You: Well, no, actually. If you wanted to learn to surf, wouldn't you go to the ocean? If you wanted to learn mountain-climbing, wouldn't you go to the mountains? If you want to learn more about faith, you should go where the faithful people are.

Jason: Man, I blew that one.

You: Forget it. Consider it a faith cramp. The point is, it makes sense to hang out with some cool Christian believers if you want to learn more about being a Christian. Find a church you really like, one with a good youth program. Also, there are a lot of great books, videos, even websites you can be loading into your mind.

Remember, just doing those things won't make you strong in your faith — just like being in a garage won't make you a car. But if you have already made a decision to pursue your faith (which really means pursuing God), then these are things you can do to help your faith become a little stronger every day.

THE FAITH WORKOUT

Use this handy list to establish the right elements to help you grow in your faith each day. You might want to ask some adults to help you fill out certain sections, like the ones on books and music.

People: These are some people I respect who can help me grow in my faith:

_____
_____
_____
_____

Books to feed my brain:

_____
_____
_____
_____

Music to feed my ears:

_____
_____
_____
_____

Websites for faith-types:

_____
_____
_____
_____

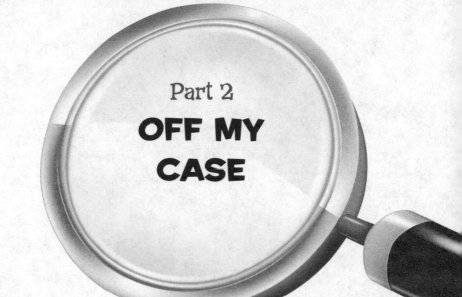

Part 2

OFF MY CASE

Sometimes there's a pretty wide gap between Sunday school lessons and real life, isn't there? On one hand, it's not hard to understand a Bible verse like 1 Peter 3:15: "Always be ready to give an answer to anyone who asks you about the hope you have." But ...

Are you ready?

Well ... maybe. But it's okay to admit that we sometimes let a chance to share our faith slip by. After all, for most of us it's hard to think of just walking up to someone and telling them how much Jesus loves them — even if we know it's true!

So that's why we're including this section of the book: some stories to help you see that everyday life is full of open doors to present the case for faith.

You'll read four short stories of everyday kids in everyday situations. You'll be able to relate to the kids and the everyday jams they get themselves into.

Oh, and if any of the stories ring a bell in other ways, that's because they're built on ideas you've already learned by reading this book.

In other words, these stories explain many of the cool ways to help us better understand Bible truths. Things like "Can I really be a Christian if I have some doubts?" These stories start with those kinds of questions, but then show us what might happen if kids draw pictures of the truth using their lives as pencils and paper.

Of course, they're not all perfect kids, and sometimes they mess up. But hey, what else is new?

As you read, imagine yourself in each of the stories. That way, you'll start seeing how everyday stuff in your own life can open the door to faith in exciting new ways. Let the stories give you ideas of your own. More important, take a couple of minutes at the end of each story to answer the Go Ahead, Stump Me! questions. Don't worry! You won't be graded, and we didn't write them to give you a hard time. But we guarantee they'll help you start thinking about how to work these ideas into your own life. After all, that's what *Case for Faith* is all about.

So have fun with the stories, and as you read them you'll discover brand-new ways to make a case for faith. And see? It's not that hard after all!

Chapter 6
Q AND A

So here's the drill, Jess," announced Matt as Jessica climbed in back next to Alyssa. He'd just picked her up in his crazy little yellow and orange and blue Volkswagen Beetle; Sarah rode in the front passenger seat.

"We're up against three other teams, and we're each going out with a video camera rolling."

So far, so good, thought Jessica. This wasn't going to be too hard.

"We're supposed to record people answering our Bible trivia questions," he added, "only we can't tell them the answers before they meet us. Everything's live on camera. It's supposed to be fun, and maybe even funny. I mean, people might say some funny things."

Okay ...

"And the first team that gets back to the youth group room at church with all twenty-five of the right answers caught on tape wins."

Unsure, Sarah said, "I'm just thinking it had better be good." She was probably afraid the rain was going to mess up her hair.

Jessica looked over at Alyssa, who always had a big-eyed expression, like she was a deer caught in the headlights. She carried a Bible everywhere she went and wore a big cross around her neck.

None of that was *bad*, of course. It was just that Sarah and Jessica were exactly like all the Christians Alyssa had ever known when she was growing up in Detroit. And she hadn't expected to find them in San Diego.

On the other hand, Matt was very cool — in fact, he was one of the main reasons Jessica became a Christian the month before and got baptized in front of everybody. He was driving them to the next place on the map, telling jokes

the whole way. He was a great guy to look up to —
kinda like a big brother.

"So there's this Sunday school teacher," he
said, "and she's trying to tell a story to her fourth-
grade class, right?"

Right. This is a joke? Jessica wondered.

"And so the teacher asks her little kids
what's little and gray, climbs trees, eats nuts, and
has a big, bushy tail."

Jessica was definitely not sure where Matt
was going with this.

"And the little kid says, 'I know the answer's
supposed to be Jesus, but it really sounds like a
squirrel to me.'"

And they all laughed, except Jessica.

*Maybe that's because they were all raised in
Sunday school*, she thought, *and I wasn't.* "I don't
get it," Jessica said carefully.

"Don't worry about it." When Matt smiled,
he had a way of making people relax. And by that
time they were pulling up to the next house anyway, so they didn't have a chance to explain the
joke to her.

But one thing Jessica was pretty good at
was asking questions. So naturally they put her
in charge of the clipboard. Matt was working
the camera, while the two other girls reviewed

directions to the next houses. Sarah was still messing with her hair.

"Whose house is this?" Alyssa wanted to know, and Jessica told her it belonged to an older couple named Al and Betty Wilson. Sounded like old people names to Jessica. But they were nice, and they were smiling when they opened the door. Pastor Jason had prepped them, so they knew the team was coming.

After the Wilsons seated themselves on the couch and the camera started rolling, Jessica asked, "And our question this time is ... what was Abraham's hometown?"

They hardly blinked, like someone had asked them who the president of the United States was.

"That would be Ur."

Mrs. Wilson smiled and squeezed her husband's hand, and he added: "Ur of the Chaldees."

Ten down, fifteen to go. They thanked the Wilsons, checked them off the list, and piled back into the Beetle.

"Hey," said Sarah, pulling down the little mirror to see if her makeup was smudged. "Maybe we're going to win the pizza party."

No one would have said that was a bad thing. Jessica wondered aloud how all those people knew the answers to so many off-the-wall Bible questions. But Alyssa just shrugged and looked at Sarah. They were raised in a Sunday school room too. And kids like that were usually the ones who said the answer was "Jesus" when the answer was really "squirrel."

The fact was, all these questions swam around in Jessica's head, making her more and more confused as the night went on. They stopped at another church person's house, and the lady who answered the door told them the answer was "the apostle Paul." Jessica told the others she didn't know very much about him, except that he was one of the twelve opossums, right? Alyssa just stared at her, like she didn't get that Jessica was just kidding.

That was Matt's joke too. Opossums. The problem was, every time she'd asked a Christian something in the past, they always looked like they were reading her some answer off a tele-prompter. You know, like TV newspeople read from. And it was always like they got mad at her for asking, like asking was a bad thing. So that's where she was coming from. But she was thinking maybe Matt was going to be different.

"So I have a question for you guys." Jessica felt brave. Or stupid, maybe. She asked herself: *What's the worst thing that can happen, right?*

"What's the story about God creating the world?" She tossed out the question, waiting to see who would snap it up. "Did it really take seven days, or longer? I've heard it both ways."

Here's where they come at me with their sound-bite answers, she thought, *and I'm going to go to hell if I don't agree with everything they say, down to the last detail that's maybe in the Bible, or maybe it's not.*

"That's a good question," answered Matt. He looked in the little rearview mirror back at Jessica, while Sarah was gagging, probably because she couldn't believe he was saying that to her. "I don't know."

Wait a minute. That wasn't an answer, was it? This was the pillar of the youth group speaking.

"What do you mean, you don't know?" Jessica asked him. "I thought Christians like you were supposed to have all the answers."

He laughed, like she was telling great jokes, which she knew she was not.

"Christians like me know where to go for the answers," he told her, "and we know what we believe. But even Christians don't always agree on everything. That's why it's okay to ask questions."

Which sounded pretty good to Jessica. But

Sarah and Alyssa rolled their eyes. They obviously disagreed with Matt.

"Matthew doesn't mean that it's actually okay," Sarah said, "I mean, to actually question your faith."

"Yes, I do." Wow. He wasn't taking anything from her. "Jesus tells us to ask, search, and knock. But even if we do, we're never going to be able to ask a question so big that God can't answer. Right?"

Okay, so this was getting pretty theological, but Jessica liked what she was hearing. By this time they were pulling up to their last house. Or it would be the last house, if they could just get the right answer from the person living there. So now Jessica was really in the question-asking mode, and Matt jumped out of the bug with his camera rolling. He ran up and pounded on the door, like there was a fire. Jessica wasn't sure about how poor Alyssa and Sarah were doing, since their boat had really been rocked.

"How many books in the Bible?" Jessica asked the young mom who answered the door.

She balanced a little kid on her hip, the way moms do. At first she looked like she wasn't going to be able to answer, but then her face lit up.

"Can I phone a friend?" she asked. And since

there wasn't anything in the rules about that, they said sure. A minute later she was talking to somebody on her cell phone.

"Sixty-six!" she yelled. "Sixty-six!"

Judging from Matt's whoop, that was the sixty-six-thousand-dollar answer, so the team yelled "Sixty-six!" all the way back to the church. Even Alyssa and Sarah got into it, since they had to be tasting the pizza too.

As they pulled up in Matt's crazy yellow and orange and blue Beetle, Jessica thought, *Maybe asking all those questions wasn't such a bad thing, after all.*

BRIEFCASE

- Going buggy. The first Volkswagen Beetle was built in Germany just before World War II, but they didn't really get into making Beetles until after the war. And they made a bunch – more than twenty-one million! For many years it was the world's most popular little car, until the last one was finally made in 2003. That's not counting the new Beetle.

- Asking the right questions at the right times is one of the best skills you can learn. Yeah, it helps you think better. But you'll be waaay better at any job if you know how to ask questions. Law enforcement? News reporting? Computers? Social work? Ministry? Whatever! Get a good book on the subject, practice, and learn to be a good questioner!

GO AHEAD, STUMP ME!

- Why is it good to ask questions, especially questions about what you believe or what the Bible teaches? (Notice the question is "Why is it GOOD ...?" Not just "Why is it OKAY ...?" There's a big difference!)

- What do you learn by asking questions, compared to what you learn when you don't?

- What questions do you have about God, or about knowing God better? Can all of your questions be answered?

Chapter 7

SOCCER MOM

Lissa smiled as her friends Natasha and Sara prayed in the corner of the locker room. This had to be one of the best parts about being on the sixth-grade girls' soccer team!

Natasha prayed for Coach Judy, that she wouldn't lose her temper (Again! Please, Lord!), while Sara prayed that all three of them would be a good witness for Jesus as they played. Well, okay — Natasha and Sara would be playing.

Lissa, short for Me-lissa (and some people said just plain short), would be warming the bench, cheering for everybody else. Oh, and she would be in charge of the first-aid kit. That's what team trainers did.

But that was okay. When it came her turn she prayed for Andrea, of course, only not out loud. Out loud she prayed that they would not get hurt and all that, in Jesus' name, amen.

And there's that moment when everybody looks up and opens their eyes, and it's usually kind of cool. A chance to catch your breath and let the prayer kind of echo around in your head before you run off to something else.

That's when Lissa heard the locker door slam right behind her. She twirled to see Andrea Romaine leaning against her locker, twirling a soccer ball on her middle finger like a circus seal, the way nobody else on the team could do.

And she was watching them.

"I don't know why you bother." Andrea's dark eyes popped a big hole in Lissa's feel-good. "If it's your karma to get hurt, you're going to get hurt. Whether you pray or not."

Karma-shmarma! Lissa would have said something to defend herself and her friends, and she would have explained how they weren't just praying not to get hurt. Really, she would have. But just then Coach Judy's voice rang out through the locker room. And they all knew there was no arguing with the coach.

"Let's go, girls! Hop to it!" Coach Judy could have been a drill sergeant, with a voice that you just couldn't ignore.

"If you get hurt, Andrea," Lissa managed, "it's nothing to do with karma."

But this was the wrong time to talk theology. All they could do was grab their water bottles and sprint out to the field. Good thing they did too, though the last girl out (Sara) got a frosty look from Coach Judy.

"You owe me three extra laps around the field next practice, Miss Pennington."

Coach Judy wasn't kidding. She would collect. But right now they had a game to play, and so they launched into warming up — stretching and sprinting and running pass-and-weave exercises.

"I want to see you MOVE!" Coach Judy even looked like a drill sergeant — as wide as she was tall, with short-short hair tucked underneath a New Jersey Wildcats cap.

But that didn't seem to scare the girls from Oak Grove Intermediate, who were getting ready at the same time on the opposite side of the field. Even from a distance they looked …

"Are those high school girls?" Natasha squinted at their opponents. "Maybe they came to the wrong field."

Sorry, but no. So Lissa didn't stop praying quietly as she watched the game start. For safety. That they wouldn't be killed. And for Andrea, who started against a towering wall of green-and-gold jerseys. In between cheers and peeking through her hands, Lissa added a PS to her prayers.

"And even if we're slaughtered, Lord," she prayed quietly, "help Andrea to see we're your kids."

That didn't seem to stop the Oak Grove girls from walking all over them, though. With cleats. *Bam-bam-bam!* Just like that, Oak Grove was leading, 3 to 0. One of the girls — who seemed to be as tall as a flagpole — sent Natasha flying as they both went for the ball.

"Aw, come on!" Lissa knew a foul when she saw it. But this time the referee didn't seem to notice, and the Oak Grove parents just cheered from the other side of the field, like they were used to winning this way. One Oak Grove mom in particular got right down on the sidelines and yelled at every player by name. Even Coach Judy noticed.

"Wow, she's pretty obnoxious," the coach noted, but under her breath. Lissa wasn't going to agree out loud, but she didn't disagree, either. Meanwhile, the soccer mom kept pacing the field, yelling out advice.

"Watch out for the little dark-haired girl!" yelled the mom.

That would be Andrea, who dived right in after the loose ball, near the goal. Would she have a shot?

"Go for it!" Lissa yelled as loudly as she could, even though the roar of the crowd drowned her out. And Lissa wasn't exactly sure how it happened, but a second later Andrea was rolling around on her back, just in front of the goal.

"Foul!" Lissa thought she'd let the referee know, just in case there had been any doubt. Meanwhile, Coach Judy streaked in to see what had happened. Lissa nearly stepped on her heels.

"You okay?" Coach Judy changed instantly from drill sergeant to nurse when her girls got hurt. She kneeled on one side of their star forward, Lissa on the other.

"Just — " Andrea looked like a fish out of water, the way her eyes kind of bulged and she couldn't seem to breathe.

"Can you walk?" Lissa blurted out. Andrea looked up at them with tears flooding her eyes. The tough-girl mask had been stripped away. So all Lissa could do was take one of Andrea's arms over her shoulder, while Coach Judy took the other. And they walked their hobbling star off the field.

"She's okay!" Coach Judy announced to everybody in the stands. "Just got the wind knocked out of her."

It was a little more than that, but the coach's words brought a round of applause as they helped Andrea to the bench and another girl took her place.

"Easy." Lissa figured a cold pack on the ankle would probably help while Andrea got her breath back.

"So much for your prayer, huh?" Andrea mumbled. "I thought God was supposed to take care of our team."

Sure, Andrea meant it as a challenge. Only this time Lissa had a pretty good idea how to answer her.

"You mean, taking care of us like the soccer mom? Yelling at us from the sidelines? That's not what my God is like."

"Hmm."

That was it? No snide comeback. No cutting remark.

Just "hmm."

Well, that was a start. And maybe Andrea didn't get it — yet. But she would. For a moment Andrea's expression softened

"So then ..." Andrea looked down at the team trainer, who was on her knees in front of the bench, holding an ice pack on her ankle. "What *is* he like?"

Lissa smiled. God *had* answered her prayer, after all.

"Thought you'd never ask."

BRIEFCASE

- Women's soccer (called "football" in the rest of the world) has been around as an organized sport since the 1930s – only not in the United States. It actually didn't catch on in the States until the 1970s, the first college teams didn't get started until the 1980s, and the first national women's team didn't organize until 1985. That's when kids who grew up playing the game started graduating to the top levels, and U.S. women's teams soon won World Cup titles and Olympic medals. Women's soccer is here to stay!

- Are there any Christians in soccer? Absolutely – and the number is growing, thanks in part to Christian ministries like Athletes in Action (AIA), Missionary Athletes International (MAI), and Ultimate Goal Ministries (UGM). AIA sends Christian workers (or team chaplains) to disciple players on various soccer teams, while MAI organizes its own teams and conducts camp outreach. UGM sends teens and young adults on short-term soccer mission trips.

- More soccer? The U.S. Youth Soccer organization organized in 1974 with just over 100,000 players. Today, it's the largest youth sports organization in the U.S., with 3.2 million registered players and more than 800,000 volunteers and coaches. No telling how many millions of kids play soccer in other countries, but it's easily the world's most popular sport.

GO AHEAD, STUMP ME!

· Why do you think God doesn't always protect us from danger?

· Does it help to pray when you or other people are in danger? Read 1 Peter 5:7 in your Bible and rethink.

· Do you think God will create something good out of something bad that happened? Does Romans 8:28 apply to this question?

· Is heaven one of those good things God created?

Chapter 8
THE GREAT TICKET SCAM

"She's okay." Megan's older brother Andrew pulled her by the sleeve through B.J. Lingbloom's front door. "You said you had extras, right?"

B.J. frowned but didn't stand in their way.

Well, what did she expect? Her brother and his friends were in ninth grade, after all. But she sure wasn't going to tell anybody she was only in sixth. No way. Maybe she looked older for her age — or she hoped so. She was almost as tall as her brother, anyway.

Still, she couldn't believe Andrew had agreed to let her come along in the first place. Maybe it was her offer to do his dishes for the next two years that sealed the deal. Were they really all going to get free passes to the new zombie movie? She couldn't tell just by looking at B.J.'s face. But now that everybody was there — B.J., Andrew, and four more high school friends that Megan didn't know — it was time to get down to business. Everybody took a seat in the Lingbloom living room. Megan balanced on the arm of a flowered love seat, waiting.

"Okay, everybody." B.J. cleared his throat and went on. "So there's good news … and there's bad news."

The other boys groaned, but B.J. held up his hands.

"Come on, you guys. First I'll tell you the bad news. The bad news is that my brother isn't coming through with the free passes like he promised."

Louder groans.

"But you said — " Andrew began.

"I know, I know." B.J. shook his head. "But he's been acting really goofy lately, ever since the born-again thing. He goes to Bible studies every morning, always talks about Jesus this and Jesus that."

Megan cringed on the inside but tried not to show it. She knew about B.J.'s brother Tyler. Actually, they'd been praying for him for months.

"Now he says I'm not going to heaven, since I don't believe the way he does." B.J. laughed. "Like there's a difference between Buddhists and Muslims and Christians, right?"

Everyone else laughed, even Megan's brother. But if *he* wasn't going to say something, she should. Not that B.J. was going to give her a chance, though.

"Yeah, but that's not even the bad part. The bad part is, now he says he can't get any more free passes for us. Says it's stealing. Can you believe it?"

"Bummer." One of the others groaned. Megan thought his name was Brian.

"Yeah," answered B.J., "but I found something in his room that I think you'll like."

He held up the prize with a grin, turning it slowly around so everyone could see the free movie pass to the Colonial Six Theater, where B.J.'s brother worked.

"But that's only one pass." Andrew told them the obvious. "And what'll your brother say if it's missing?"

Megan would have asked the same thing if she'd had enough guts.

B.J. dropped his jaw too much, like he was acting.

"You don't actually think I'd *steal* this from my dear old born-again brother, do you?"

Megan gulped again. Had she really begged her brother to let her come?

But B.J. wasn't done, and with a smile he picked up a stack of stiff construction paper from the coffee table.

"Hey, I'm not a bad person." The grin never left B.J.'s face. "All I'm going to do is *borrow* my brother's free pass for a few minutes so we can make our own free passes."

Finally it was sinking in, and by this time Megan's eyes must have given her away. B.J. looked straight at her.

"You want to see the movie, right?"

She nodded.

"Okay, so don't worry about it. It's not hurting anybody, and we're not stealing anything. Hey, it's kind of like getting into heaven, right?" He grinned and acted as if he'd just come up with a great new spiritual truth. "Our passes are going to be as good as anybody else's passes. They'll get us in, no problem, Morgan."

"Megan." She couldn't believe she was correcting him, almost as much as she couldn't believe he was talking to her.

"Megan, right. You know how to use a scanner to make copies?"

Well, she did. And even though the voice in the back of her mind said *no-no-no*, she helped the boys scan the free pass on B.J.'s flatbed scanner. The paper they used to print ten passes looked and felt almost the same as the real thing. It didn't take long.

"Hey, pretty cool!" Brian held their phony passes up to the light. "Anybody want to try dollar bills? Just kidding!"

Good thing. But Megan tried to keep her hand from shaking as she cut out the counterfeits they'd made. What was she doing?

"Which one's the original?" her brother asked her. She had to search through the pile of paper, though, and even then she still wasn't sure.

"Yeah, it'll work." Once again B.J. was in charge as they gathered up the passes and slapped one another on the back. "And Morgan's going to prove it for us."

This time Megan didn't ask too many questions, only closed her eyes and nodded. Too late now, right?

Whether it was or not, an hour later she was moving up in line at the Colonial Six, clutching her fake pass and sweating. She glanced behind her to make sure Andrew, B.J., and the others were still following, the way they'd planned. If it worked for her, they'd all be in the clear. So she moved ahead, feeling like a fool.

"I'm sorry, Lord," she whispered, her eyes closed, wondering what would happen if she turned and ran. Suddenly she wasn't so sure she wanted to see this movie that much.

"Pardon?"

The ticket-taker looked at her with a puzzled expression, his hand held out.

"Oh, sorry. Nothing." She swallowed hard and gave him the pass, which he tried to scan with a handheld scanner.

But it kept going *boop* and flashing a red light. This was not good.

"That's odd." The ticket guy kept trying as a manager-looking lady came up to help. She tried the scanner, which didn't work for her, either. Megan wanted to scream. Out of the corner of her eye she could see the boys heading for the door.

Thanks a lot, guys, she thought.

"Where did you get this?" By this time the manager lady was looking closely at the pass, especially the corner where the ink had smudged from Megan's sweaty hand. To make matters worse, a couple of Megan's friends from school waved at her from the other line.

"See you inside, Megan!" said Antonia Parris as she headed for the snack counter.

At least it looked like Antonia. Megan couldn't tell through her tears. And they were real too, unlike the fake pass. Unlike the older boys who had set her up.

Not that she blamed them, really. Not even her brother, the coward. She'd been the same way. Now she only blamed herself — for letting herself get sucked into this whole ugly mess. And as she walked between a security guard and the manager on their way to the manager's office and more trouble, she could still remember B.J.'s hollow promise: *Our passes are going to be as good as anybody else's passes. They'll get us in, no problem.*

Only, where was B.J. now?

BRIEFCASE

- The biggest. What are the top five movies of all time in the U.S., based on how much money they made? If you figure out how much a movie ticket really cost in yesterday's dollars, the top Films are *Gone with the Wind* (1939), *Star Wars* (1977), *The Sound of Music* (1965), *E.T.* (1982), and *The Ten Commandments* (1956), in that order.

- Christian movies. What is a Christian movie, anyway? A story about Christians? A Bible story? Or a story told by a Christian? This actually is not an easy question, and Christians don't seem to agree on the answers. One thing is sure, though: more and more Christians are getting involved in filmmaking, and they're starting to make their mark. *The Passion of the Christ* is one approach. Look for more as young Christian moviemakers (maybe like you?) get more and more creative.

- Peel your potato. In the classic film *Chariots of Fire*, Scottish Olympic runner Eric Liddel wonders how he can be a Christian and an athlete too. His father tells him, "You can glorify God by peeling a potato if you peel it to perfection." That's good advice for us too! (By the way, after winning his medals, the true-life Eric Liddel went on to be a missionary in China.)

GO AHEAD, STUMP ME!

· Do you think other religions can get you into heaven? Why or why not? What does Jesus say about this in John 14:6?

· The way B.J. saw it, getting into heaven was sort of like sneaking into a movie. Explain what he believed, and why it didn't work.

· Why didn't Megan say what she believed when she had a chance? Have you ever felt the same way? What could you do about it in the future?

Chapter 9

PFD MEANS "PRETTY FAT DUMMY"

Ah, the smell of the lake at sunset. Ah, the call of the loons. Ah, the ...

"We're going in circles again, Franklin."

Gilbert was right. But even though Franklin tried to paddle on the other side, it didn't do any good. Surprise! They were hopeless, all right, and everybody at Silver Lake Camp knew it.

Especially Keith Olderman and Chris Rio, who could have towed a water-skier behind their canoe if they'd wanted to. As they cruised by, the wave they made behind them seemed like it would tip Gilbert and Franklin's boat over.

"Hey, it's the PFD boys!" Keith shouted across the water at them. By that time, he was so close he didn't need to raise his voice. "We all know what that stands for, right? Although, Franklin, I'm surprised they make a life jacket that actually fits you!"

"Knock it off, Keith." Chris laughed and pretended to scold his friend. He stood up and rode the canoe like a surfer on a board. "They're just doing exactly what their Sunday school teacher told them to. Say your prayers every day and stay out of deep water. Right, Gilly-bert?"

Franklin flinched when an icy spray of cold water hit him square in the face. Keith smacked his paddle again, sending a shower over Franklin and Gilbert. Chris cackled even harder.

"The water's really cold, guys." Gilbert mopped his face with his sleeve. "And you really ought to wear your life jackets. You know the lifeguard would ground you if he saw."

A person would have to know Gilbert to understand that he never said anything mean to irritate anyone. He was just bringing it up because he didn't want Keith and Chris to get hurt or in trouble, period.

"Awww ..." This time Chris laid it on extra thick. "The choirboys are a wittle bit gwumpy, and now they're going to tell on us."

Franklin bit his tongue and waited for Gilbert to say something. Instead, Chris slapped the water with his paddle once again, sending a wave that made Gilbert duck and almost tip the canoe.

"Gilbert!" Franklin tried to balance the canoe from the front but only managed to slosh a few gallons over the side. Yeah, it was a good thing they were wearing their PFDs — personal flotation devices. They might be needing them soon.

Keith and Chris wouldn't be coming to the rescue, though. They'd already paddled away and were on their way to harass somebody else. "Time to turn back?" asked Franklin, and Gilbert nodded quietly. It was already getting a little misty on the lake as Keith's laugh echoed across the water.

Only this time they managed to paddle in time with each other, Franklin on one side, Gilbert on the other. Franklin in front, Gilbert in the back. All it took was a little more practice.

"I'm sorry about all that, Gil." Franklin leaned forward as far as he could, though it wasn't quite enough to keep his end of the canoe all the way in the water.

"About what?" Gilbert asked between breaths. As if they both didn't know.

"Oh, come on. The PFD thing. Kids always teasing you about your size."

And it was true. His friend had to be at least fifty pounds overweight. But when Franklin looked back over his shoulder, Gilbert only shook his head.

"That's not what bugs me so much," replied Gilbert.

"Then what?"

"It's all the 'choirboy' and 'Sunday school' junk. Just because you and I are the only guys in our cabin who brought our Bibles to camp, we're ... well, you heard it. It gets kinda old."

Sure it did, but Franklin was glad he could hang around with somebody who understood. It helped when the little doubts started to creep into the back of his mind. They talked about their doubts as they paddled on for the next hour. The wind started to whip up little waves, and the sun disappeared behind the woodsy western shore of Silver Lake. They talked about youth group at church, and what they might do or say the next time Keith and Chris got nasty. About girls. About what was for dinner. As they neared the swimming area, Franklin figured the other boys must have slipped in already.

They quickened their stroke when they saw the lifeguard standing on the dock, arms crossed and obviously waiting for them.

"Are we in trouble?" asked Gilbert.

Franklin wasn't sure. They were probably the last ones to return, but the lifeguard didn't even give them a chance to find out.

"You seen Keith and Chris?" the lifeguard yelled. "They should have been back an hour ago."

"We saw them go back that way!" Franklin pointed to the far side of the lake, where it widened out and the wind was the strongest. Without even talking about it, they turned the boat around and headed out once more.

"We'll show you!" Gilbert called back.

"My boat motor won't start," replied the lifeguard, "but I've got a call in to the sheriff to see if he can put a boat out there. I'll be right behind you with a light."

Franklin ignored the ache across his shoulders from the past several hours of paddling, digging in and pulling as he never had before. Behind him, Gilbert did the same. And in the growing darkness he could also hear Gilbert softly praying. Finally at the darkened west shore, they paused to listen.

"Hear anything?" Franklin thought the

loudest thing had to be his heart pounding. But besides the waves slapping their little boat, they heard only wind whistling across the lake and through the pines — and a distant shout?

"That way?" In the darkness Franklin couldn't be sure. Neither could Gilbert. They circled once and made their way toward the middle of Beaver Bay, full speed ahead. Gasping for air, Franklin saw the lifeguard's light flickering behind them, though it was farther away than he'd expected.

They nearly ran over what Franklin thought might be a rock. But than he saw a flicker of moonlight reflected off a pale, scared face looking up at them from the waves. Chris could barely raise his hand above the water, but Franklin grabbed it and held on tight. Keith gripped the side of their boat too, but at least he knew enough not to try to climb aboard and swamp them. Neither was wearing his PFD.

"Our boat tipped," croaked Chris. "But man, am I glad to see you guys, 'cause ..."

He couldn't finish; his teeth were chattering too much. But it didn't matter, and Franklin didn't have time to think about how odd those words sounded. Keith and Chris — actually glad to see the choirboys? Well, they could talk later.

For now it was enough to thank God, hold on to Chris's cold hands, and wait for the lifeguard's boat to catch up.

BRIEFCASE

- Boating accidents without PFDs. The U.S. Coast Guard reports that a few years ago, 524 people died in boating accidents. Of those, 442 were not wearing life jackets! Seriously, the Coast Guard thinks that nine out of ten drownings could be avoided if people would just wear life jackets.

- Do you canoe? The native peoples of North America first came up with the idea for a canoe. They perfected their designs over many years, from hollowed-out tree trunks in the Caribbean islands to kayaks in the far North and the more traditional birch-bark canoe in between. The word *canoe* comes from the native word *kenu*, which means "dugout."

- Embarrassed for Jesus? If you think it's getting tough to be a Christian in North America, consider the alternative: Tribal Christians in the hills of Vietnam are being persecuted as never before. It's hard to follow Jesus in most Muslim countries without facing jail ... or even the death sentence. And Christians in the underground church in China can't worship together in their own homes without the police coming to arrest them!

GO AHEAD, STUMP ME!

· What would you say to someone who made fun of you for being a Christian? What would you do, if you had a chance? (And don't say, "I'd put ants in their bed"!)

· Could cruel comments or name-calling make you question your faith, the way it did for Franklin in the story? What if it did?

· Name three steps you can take to keep your faith strong and healthy. (Hint: What did Franklin and Gilbert do that set them apart? How did they react to Chris and Keith, and what did they do for them?)

Did you get it?

What's at the top of the page, that's what! Did you get it?

It says, "The Beginning." Get it? This part of the book is usually called "The End," but not in this book! Here it's called "The Beginning." Isn't that a riot?

You don't think so?

Okay, well, if you're so smart, maybe you can make up a better title for the last chapter. Just cross out our title and write in your own. Because you know what? That's kind of what this part of the book is about anyway: crossing out stuff and writing in your own. We're talking about questions, answers, growth, and *faith*.

In these pages you worked through some of the big questions people have about believing in God. The questions were set up and knocked down. You learned a lot about what experts have studied and learned about faith and God. In every case, these people have built a stronger faith and happier lives.

Now it's time for you to start your own journey. That's why this chapter is called "The Beginning: Where to Next?" Because books run out of pages. Because writers run out of words. Because the time comes when you have to take the ball and run with it.

So, where to now?

MULTIPLE CHOICE

What are your options? Well, there are a bunch. You could join any of the following groups:

DENIERS, who reject the whole idea of God.

DELAYERS, who believe in God but never get started on the journey.

DEPARTERS, who start the journey but never get too far.

DELIGHTERS, who get going and travel with excitement.

You're going to meet a lot of people in your lifetime. A few of them will be **DENIERS,** who chuck the whole idea of God and faith. Deniers say things like, "Why would I need God? I live the way I want," or, "It's all foolish superstition."

There are plenty of **DELAYERS** too. When you meet them, they're likely to say something like, "Sure, I suppose there's probably some kind of God or creative Spirit out there." But Delayers are in no hurry to set out on the journey to find out for sure. They live very much like the first group, actually.

DEPARTERS grab their coats and say, "Sounds great; let's go!" when you invite them on the journey of faith. But they get distracted. They have trouble staying on the path. These are people who believe in God and have a little faith, but they haven't taken it very far.

Finally, there are a few people out there who are **DELIGHTERS**. They are delighted with God.

They are delighted with their faith. They are delighted when they see new evidence from science and history that makes their faith even stronger. And they delight God too. They believe in the verse that says, "Find your delight in the Lord. Then he will give you everything your heart really wants" (Psalm 37:4). For them, life is a journey of adventure, with something new and exciting every day. Their eyes are set on something in the distance, as if they see a wonderful destination at the end of the road. Listen to what the Bible says about them:

> What if they had been thinking of the country they had left? Then they could have returned to it. Instead, they longed for a better country. They wanted one in heaven. So God is pleased when they call him their God. In fact, he has prepared a city for them.
> (Hebrews 11:15–16)

Question: Which of the four D's describes you best? Which category would you like to be a part of? Why?

NEW QUESTIONS

If you choose to place yourself in that final category — those who travel the journey of faith with delight — you may very well continue to have some questions. But some of the questions will be new ones. You'll have questions such as:

- How can I learn even more about God?
- How can I please him even more?
- How can I invite some of my friends to make the journey with me?

That last question is a good one. Because whenever we discover something really awesome, we are eager to share it with friends. You might even start by sharing this book with a friend. Then you can talk together about some of the ideas in here.

But look! Space is running out. It's time for you to get going. Have a great trip. Enjoy every moment. Bring along your best questions and a good, God-given mind to think them over with. You're going to have a great time, because there's one thing about this trip: It's not just the destination that's fantastic. The journey is wonderful too. It's filled with hope, new friends along the way, and new things to learn all the time. Best of all is realizing that when you get to the end of the trail, all of your questions will be fully answered.

Case for ... Series for Kids
from Lee Strobel

Case for Christ for Kids, Updated and Expanded

Lee Strobel

You meet skeptics every day. They ask questions like:

Was Jesus really born in a stable?

Did his friends tell the truth?

Did he really come back from the dead?

Here's a book written in kid-friendly language that gives you all the answers.

Packed full of well-researched, reliable, and eye-opening investigations of some of the biggest questions you have, *Case for Christ for Kids* brings Christ to life by addressing the existence, miracles, ministry, and resurrection of Jesus of Nazareth.

Pick up a copy at your favorite bookstore or online!